Mission Accompaniment

Lessons from Building Bridges of Hope

Philip Walker

Founder, Healthy Church UK
Natural Church Development Partner for the UK and Ireland

GROVE BOOKS LIMITED
RIDLEY HALL RD CAMBRIDGE CB3 9HU

Contents

The Cover Illustration is by Peter Ashton

First Impression February 2005
ISSN 1367-0840
ISBN 1 85174 585 5

Introduction 1

As an 'outsider' I want to commend the principle of 'mission accompaniment' from the project Building Bridges of Hope (BBH).

It is, I believe, a biblical model and invaluable tool in helping local churches and projects in their mission journey.

In brief, the accompanier is not an expert telling a group what to do, just someone who is a skilful outsider, who encourages and accompanies the church or project in developing its mission.

The last Grove Evangelism book, *How to Develop a Mission Strategy*[1] commends the 'Mission Enabler,' and many evangelists and mission consultants provide an invaluable service to congregations in developing their mission potential. This work will look at 'accompanying' in more detail, based on four very different stories from BBH.

My own work with a wide variety of churches considering the Natural Church Development process[2] demonstrates that churches that have outside help are far more effective in producing change than those that rely totally on their own resources.

I well remember visiting for a consultation a church which had a strange attendance pattern. Over 20 years they had increased to about 100, and then gone back to 20, three times. As I arrived at the church a little early I walked through the door, and could see at least part of the problem—there were no more than 100 chairs! When they had been full they considered it a great joy, but they did not take steps to go on growing, and decline was the result.

Churches that have outside help are far more effective in producing change

In 2000 I was introduced to the Churches Together in Britain and Ireland initiative commonly called Building Bridges of Hope (BBH). Invited to join the new Four-Nation Development Group, I saw exciting developments and realized that 'mission accompaniment' is the most important aspect of the work. Someone who has had a BBH Mission Accompanier as a part of the ongoing learning process wrote:

> The accompaniment has been very helpful, as he has been able to see an overview of the process and guide and encourage the group to realize the visions we have. He was able to lead us in identifying those visions and values that we had and the gifts we had to implement them. He was able to focus a small group of inexperienced lay people into a church council, which is growing and working on the ground. He moved us on from a vision group to a steering committee to a building committee (for our new church and community building) to a church council.

The accompanier made all the difference to this group of people, and it is this process that I want to explore, examine and assess. Before we do that, let me share the first story with you.

Story 1: Newtown CTYÛN[3]

Story told by Matt Kruczek, local Church Army Evangelist in the Church in Wales.
On the banks of a still-young river Severn, at the meeting point of the main north-south and east-west roads in Wales, lies Newtown, home to 13,000 people. It has an astonishing concentration of fifteen places of worship serving the town, ten of which fit in an area no larger than the Millennium Stadium. There was, and still is, a lot of ecumenical and mission work to be done.

In 2001, Newtown CYTÛN began the process of becoming a BBH pilot. The broad aim was to improve relationships—within congregations, between congregations and beyond that into the wider community.

Church life has been described as 'People talking to people about a person—Jesus,'[4] whereas ecumenical life in Newtown, as in many other places, had become institutions talking to institutions about how they were going to talk to each other.

The process of accompaniment formally began in early 2002. The style and atmosphere were relaxed, but not unchallenging. The accompanier was happy to let discussions flow and be directed by the chair of the group, but was not afraid to interject a demanding or stimulating question or comment, as the situation required it.

Within the group, there were some expectations that the accompanier would act as an expert and provide answers and solutions to the situation, to 'tell us what to do.' Whilst this is a common belief in many churches regarding 'outside help,' here it was also reflective of a broader mood throughout all the churches and chapels of a disempowered laity, expecting, even demanding, to do very little while clergy and other recognized ministers did 'the work of church.'

During the three years of the accompaniment process, the steering group met once a month, with the accompanier being present at every other meeting. This allowed the group to get on with the nuts-and-bolts everyday organization on its own, and to spend time in reflection and envisioning with the accompanier. The most helpful thing was the opportunity to ask searching and critical questions about what CYTÛN was actually doing. Looking back it is clear that the reason why CYTÛN was calcifying was that for a long time no one had thought to ask the question 'Why?' Not only did accompaniment provide CYTÛN with that opportunity, it forced it into answering the question too.

One of the most exciting and encouraging events to take place during the period of accompaniment was '24–7.' This was a week of non-stop, concentrated prayer open to all denominations. For seven days over fifty people took turns to maintain a continuous presence in a specially adapted room in one of the Anglican churches. Numerous ways of engaging in prayer were on offer, from the simple to the creative, the traditional to the modern. People who, by their own admission, had never really prayed on their own before, found themselves easily praying for the allocated hour they had signed up for…and then put themselves down for two hours later in the week.

Folk from all the denominations were not only discovering the power of prayer, but also the power and sense of unity that comes from praying *together*. That sense of prayerful togetherness seemed to be what the churches and chapels had been missing and craving. Next year it was repeated.

Where the first 24–7 had been about people discovering prayer, the second seemed to be about bringing people together. People from every church and chapel were seeing the potential of what could be achieved with greater co-operation. We began to realize what the churches and chapels were capable of, and how much the existing CYTÛN structures needed to change to allow that to happen.

There has been greater difficulty in turning that desire into concrete action. An initial vision of a cross-denominational cell church stalled twice, partially due to a CYTÛN that would nod its agreement to the idea at the quarterly meetings, but would not promote, support or encourage it in their individual churches week by week. A few people from the BBH steering group have been taking part in a cell belonging to the local Salvation Army, and they have had a very positive experience, frequently commenting that cell is the type of community that CYTÛN should be striving to be. One member of the cell writes:

BBH has modelled Jesus to the group, encouraging us to use our individual gifts given by God and allowing our spiritual gifts to develop in a climate of trust and security. Jesus has been involved in our meetings, allowing us to share everything we have in common, always with Jesus at the centre.

BBH has been a community of honest, open, sacrificial relationships where I have grown and wanted to be more like Jesus. I have been allowed to take part to contribute to church life and discipleship, serving Jesus with others' help, because of the mutual love and respect found in the meetings, and the importance of prayer and the desire to worship Jesus together, and then serve him.

As the period of accompaniment drew to a close, it was widely and keenly felt that the experiences of being accompanied, of building networks and of nourishing daily living needed to be communicated to the wider CYTÛN community. It was also noted that delivering a written or spoken report to a quarterly meeting would not be able adequately to put across the value and experience. So, at the suggestion of the BBH steering group, CYTÛN as a whole will have an accompanier for the near future, with the intention of moving all Christians in Newtown forward in mission together.

Comment

What a great result—but my immediate question is whether this would have happened anyway. The heart for change was already there and the people were in place to see it happen, for they were the ones negotiating to become the BBH pilot. What then was the role of the accompanier? Clearly, as the name implies, it is to accompany others in *their* journey, but more of that later. I think the story of Newtown highlights two aspects:

1 Accompaniment does seem to make a real difference in people's lives as (for example) the cell member reports.

2 This is *mission* accompaniment. It is not accompaniment just to show some improvement in a given situation; its *raison d'etre* is both change and *mission*.

You may be aware of the BBH research project already, but if not, this story has used terms which have not yet been explained, so let us explore these by looking at the basics of what BBH is all about. After that we shall then look at 'accompaniment' again, and how it might be helpful in your context.

The History of BBH 2

As previously mentioned BBH is an initiative of Churches Together in Britain and Ireland. It is currently in Stage C of its development.

Stage A

Stage A began with an extensive visitation of a wide variety of local churches, which led to consultations among the national churches. These confirmed the value of and commitment to a locally focused project to discover practical ways for churches to move from maintenance to mission and from self-engagement to a more effective engagement with their local communities.

Stage B

Stage B examined some 40 different local churches across Britain and Ireland from Catholic to Pentecostal. These diverse groups were accompanied, observed, and researched over a three-year period. The aim was to examine a broad range of models and experiences, without any of them having a prior claim to being especially successful.

At this stage a great deal of evidence was gathered and analyzed. From this seven key learning indicators of a mission church emerged:

1 *Focusing Vision.* The importance of local churches articulating their specific calling through integrated strategies for community engaging, mature spiritual life, enabling leadership and appropriate structure.

2 *Building Local Partnerships.* The significance of seeking and forming partnerships of action with those with similar concerns in the wider community inside and outside the church.

3 *Sharing Faith and Values.* A commitment to exploring respectful and creative ways to share values, aspirations and faith in and beyond church circles in relation to the gospel story.

4 *Nourishing Daily Living.* The critical need for believers old and new to relate biblical faith to personal life, work and culture in society today, through worship and reflection.

5 *Developing Shared Leadership.* The importance of forming in context (clergy–lay and other forms) team leadership which is animated by one another, and linked to both church learning institutions and to genuine community participation.

6 *Becoming Communities of Learning.* Churches at every level need to become places where the lessons about how to be 'bridge-builders' with others can be developed, consolidated and extended.

7 *A Willingness to be Accompanied.* The value of welcoming systematic accompaniment and evaluation in non-directive ways from beyond the local—and the sharing of stories and experience in order to be able to look at each other with fresh eyes.

Stage C

Stage C, the present stage, began to extend the research from local churches into a range of pilot situations that start from, but extend beyond, the local. They include projects in dioceses, deaneries, provinces, churches together bodies, projects, action zones, experimental groups and training institutions. It is important to note that these are places where initiatives were already underway—BBH does not impose ideas or activities from the outside, but it accompanies groups already on the journey.

BBH does not impose ideas or activities from the outside, but it accompanies groups already on the journey

Over the past four years it has become clear that out of the seven indicators, the one which marks out BBH (its unique selling point or USP if you like!) is mission accompaniment. That has not meant that the other six are unimportant or insignificant; it is just that the outside help—the mission accompaniment—has become the most important part of the process.

I now use the term 'mission accompanier' much of the time, but you could easily replace it with the term co-journeyer, coach or consultant (although each one has slight differences). In Stage B, the term 'participant observer' was used, but the accompaniment that has developed is a little more than that, although this remains a good description of much that takes place.

What is Mission Accompaniment? 3

I hope by now you have begun to catch a flavour of mission accompaniment, but what are the particular distinctives of BBH accompaniment?

- It uses *ecumenical* (cross-church) mission accompaniers who are in sympathy with the pilot church. This difference provides fresh eyes and the opportunity to ask both naïve questions that those within may be diffident to ask, and challenging questions relating to purpose, values and vision.
- It is *long-term* accompaniment—the process is an enduring one that permits sustainable change and development to take place in an environment of trust, encouragement, and experience by having the friendly and skilful outsider alongside.
- The primary methods of accompaniment begin with *listening to the context*, both what is said and what is not said. *Catalytic questions* allow for action reflection and joined up thinking in terms of how a mission statement is integrated in the weekly life of church. *Suggestive options and signposting* of other resources are encouraged, whilst always keeping the church at the centre of responsible decision-making.
- BBH accompaniers are both *process focused* in accompaniment and *have specialist knowledge* to add value in assisting churches in mission engagement in the community.

An example of this process from the point of view of the accompanier, John Ledger, and the people being accompanied will help our understanding.

Story 2: Bridges Centre in Edenbridge, Kent

Story told by John Ledger, BBH Accompanier, lay Anglican.
Bridges is a registered charity established by lay members of churches in Edenbridge for the advancement of the Christian faith and in particular to establish and maintain an ecumenical centre there.

The core aim is to build bridges between all sections of the community (hence the name adopted) as an expression of the social mission of the Christian church and to develop the listening mission of lay people. That aim is advanced through two main projects, the Bridges Centre in Edenbridge High Street, and the Allsorts Children's Club on a London overspill estate.

The Centre's core activity is a pop-in centre and subsidiary activities include youth, art and other projects. Allsorts is an after-school club providing subsidized, supervised play facilities and out-of-school and holiday care for children aged 4–15. It primarily serves disadvantaged parents and children.

> ### My Aims as Accompanier
> a) To assist Bridges to fulfil their own aims to be a meaningful and relevant Christian presence in Edenbridge;
> b) To explore the applicability of three or four of the BBH indicators to Bridges;
> c) To see what can be taken from the Bridges experience to help and encourage other projects seeking to be 'church' in the community.

Manner and Style of Accompaniment

Initially there was the need to build up a relationship of trust and friendship so that I could 'walk with them' and honestly comment on what I saw. My first visit to the Bridges pop-in centre was anonymous (I was meeting a trustee later). The experience was not particularly welcoming, and the volunteer serving at the counter was more interested in speaking to the person in the kitchen. After sitting down with my meal, I looked around to see if there were any indication as to whether this was a Christian place. The only clue was some little booklets in a rack by the door whose covers I recognized from having used them in other places. I was quite relieved when the trustee eventually arrived and I felt less lost in a strange place in a strange town! Subsequently I was sensitively able to feed back this experience to the trustees at a meeting. Wisdom is required to know when to let them do something their way or point (steer) them in what might be a more effective direction for their project. There have been moments when it has seemed appropriate to be more active than passive in my approach.

The accompaniment is ongoing at the time of writing, and it is true to say that my original aims are being fulfilled.

Initially I visited Bridges Centre and Allsorts, attended their respective management committees and visited local clergy to ascertain their views on the project. Then at the beginning of 2002, I started attending trustees' meetings as this appeared to be the appropriate group to work with on a regular basis. I attend approximately every two months, as well as on special occasions, such as the AGM and the official opening of the refurbished Centre.

This has allowed the trustees to reassess their original aims (formulated ten years ago) and to sharpen up on their implementation of them, particularly concerning sharing faith and values, as a key priority during the refurbishment of the Centre which took place during 2002/3.

Successes and Failures

One positive outcome is the trustees, as project leaders, have grasped that they are 'church' in the community (not just a centre or club) and have a real role to play, complementing the work of the traditional churches in the town. Fortunately, the local clergy and ministers accept this and do not seem to consider Bridges as a 'threat' to their own work. I have encouraged Bridges to exploit their Christian distinctiveness as a facility on the High Street, being where ordinary people are!

Another success has been to enable them to see what they are actually doing rather than just having aims on paper.

On the other hand, the speed of progress has been much slower than anticipated. This is partly due to the refurbishment programme taking 16 rather than 6 months, and difficulties put in their path becoming their chief priority.

The management of the Allsorts project has lurched from one crisis to another. This project, which was taken under the wing of Bridges, seeks to help children with behavioural difficulties. The supervisor and helpers, who are able to relate to and deal with the children, have little concept of managing a project. The trustees have been able to supply some of the missing elements, but there still remains a serious gap.

Considering the BBH Indicators

The most helpful of the seven indicators was Sharing Faith and Values, as this is at the very heart of this project (see aims above). They were prompted to consider carefully how this could be implemented in practice by Centre staff and volunteers. For instance, they recognized the need to make this a priority for all, and ideally to have a person on each shift whose primary role is to be a 'befriender' of visitors as appropriate.

The least helpful of the indicators were Developing Shared Leadership and Becoming Communities of Learning. Bridges is not a church-based project, but nonetheless does operate in partnership with Edenbridge Churches in Covenant.

The Future of the Project

The main expectations for the future of the project are:

- That the Bridges Centre will be truly 'church' for people in Edenbridge who would not attend or even seek to make contact with a local church.

- That secular organizations and statutory authorities will appreciate the advantages of working in partnership with Bridges as a result of the ethos and values, which it represents.

The Local Response to the Mission Accompanier

Some of the people working with Bridges have thought about their response to this process and have said:

> John has helped us recognize the extent to which the original vision has not been fully absorbed by new volunteers, and the consequent perception that 'Christian' ministry is left to the original helpers rather than being something that everyone can be engaged in, at their own level of comfort.

> John has met Bridges at a low ebb. The tasks he has set us have felt hard, but without this process of review, we might not have asked ourselves the hard questions, nor admitted that things were not always as successful or as fruitful as we would have liked to believe. We have been prone to looking back at a 'golden age,' when everything was new and 'taking off.' The review has looked at where we are now. It has identified the strengths and potential of Allsorts, our 'adopted' project as being comparable to those of the Bridges Centre, our 'firstborn' offspring.

> John has identified our low-key Christian witness as an area for reassessment. While we have not wanted to change the principle of befriending being the first stage of evangelism, we have been challenged by the question 'How do people know that this is a Christian project?'

> This may have seemed an awful time to do the BBH review as the Centre has been out of commission for almost the whole period. On the other hand, if we had not had John alongside us during this period

Biblical Examples of Accompaniment

The Paraclete

I was challenged recently when reading an interview with Bill Hybels on preaching. He says, 'When I am in the flow of the Spirit as best I can yield myself to be so, it's as though I have an awareness of the *accompanying presence* of the Spirit.'[5] That set me thinking!

Would it be wrong to see the Holy Spirit in this way? I do not think so! John is the only New Testament writer to use the term 'paraclete' of the Holy Spirit (John 14.26, 15.26, 16.7, 1 John 2.1), but although it is never translated 'accompanier' that could easily be the meaning. Let me explain.

The older translations of the Bible translate the word 'Comforter' following Wycliffe and then Tyndale, which seems inadequate for today's understanding of the word. In Wycliffe's time, the meaning was probably much nearer to 'helper' as the word is derived from *con* and *fortis*, and means, etymologically, to encourage or strengthen. So modern translations use words like 'Counsellor' (NIV), 'Friend' (Msg) or even 'Advocate' (ESV). The word literally means someone who comes alongside and so it is easy to see why these translations are used, but is that not what an accompanier does?

However, if this is a true understanding, John suggests several functions for the Paraclete:

1 He is a teacher (14.26)
2 He reminds us of old truths, especially the teaching of Jesus (14.26, 15.26)
3 He brings the gift of peace (14.27)
4 He defends our cause (1 John 2.1)

Clearly the Holy Spirit will (and does) do this perfectly. It may help us to understand accompaniment better by seeing these aspects as a part of the process. If the Holy Spirit does all this, is a third party superfluous? The biblical principle I see is that God primarily works through human beings. As a part of his body, we are his hands and feet.

> *Question:* Could John's suggested functions for the Paraclete be our model for accompaniment?

Other Biblical References

You will look in vain for direct biblical references to accompaniment, as it is understood in the BBH process. Of course, unscrupulous exegetes might refer to 1 Corinthians 16.4 or 2 Corinthians 8.19, where the NIV uses the verb 'accompany' but not the noun, although there is an element of this in BBH accompaniment—travelling with the group. Indeed, in Scotland they have preferred the term 'co-journeyer.' Paul is simply referring to people going with him and no more, so to use these as proof texts would be to stretch the text. So where do we go? I would suggest that the following examples might help us to see some of the principles at work.

Jethro and Moses (Exodus 18)
Moses was so involved with the work that he failed to see what was going on. It took an outsider, in this case his father-in-law, to realize the problem and suggest a solution. It is to Moses' credit that he listened and acted on what was being said. This illustrates well one of the principles of accompaniment.

Question: Who acts as your 'Jethro,' and points out what is really going on?

Jesus with Peter, James and John
These three disciples seem to have formed an inner circle of the Twelve and Mark records three events where Jesus singles them out for special mentoring (Mark 5.37; 9.2; 14.33[6]). When the daughter of Jairus was healed, he would not let anyone else follow him—only these three were with him when he was transfigured and Jesus chose these three to be with him as he prayed on the night of his betrayal. They were clearly being prepared for significant leadership roles in the period that followed the Day of Pentecost, so Jesus gave them significant support, encouragement and training above the other nine disciples—he accompanied them! In Galatians 2.9, Paul describes these three as 'those reputed to be pillars' who gave Paul and Barnabas the right hand of fellowship and agreed that they should go to the Gentiles while these three continued their work amongst the Jews.

Question: Are you mentoring special people for leadership in the future?

The Road to Emmaus
The story of Jesus walking with the two going from Jerusalem to the village of Emmaus is an illustration of accompaniment. The two were sorrowfully discussing the events of the previous few days, and all that had gone before, when Jesus simply joined them and walked with them. This would not be a strange thing to do, but he began by asking a simple question, and from there he began to explain the Scriptures. So what might we understand from this event?

- He was unobtrusive as he arrived, just a stranger who was on the same road.
- He walked with them and began to enter into their story.

- He became a part of this small group and was able to give them input.
- He took them much further than they realized, but as they looked back after he revealed himself to them, they knew what had been happening. Their journey back to Jerusalem was very different from the journey to Emmaus!

Question: As you look back, have there been people who have come alongside you quietly and gently and have changed your outlook?

Barnabas and Saul

Barnabas sought out Saul when he was sent to Antioch. I suppose he could have gone on his own, but I think there were two things in his mind—Saul was an excellent teacher and could help the work in Antioch and he also needed a wider audience so this could be his period of development. It took a big man to hand over the leadership of the ministry, but this is what Barnabas certainly did. He did not consider the leadership of the ministry something to be grasped, but handed it over for the sake of the greater ministry. There is a great lesson there. The ministry is of far greater importance than personal status or gain. It may well have been Barnabas' training that set Paul on his path of seeking others to go with him throughout the rest of his ministry.

Question: Do you 'hold on' to leadership or are you willing to hand it over like Barnabas?

Paul and His Other Co-workers

It seems that Paul never liked to be alone! After falling out with Barnabas, he immediately teamed up with Silas. Then there was Timothy and the many people listed at the end of his letters, who all accompanied him during part of his journey. The Western trait is to try to do everything ourselves. Perhaps we need to learn from Paul. His constant desire for individuals and churches is expressed in Colossians 2.2: 'My purpose is that they may be encouraged in heart and united in love, so that they may have the full riches of complete understanding, in order that they may know the mystery of God, namely, Christ.'

Question: What kind of ongoing accompaniment do you have?

Paul and the Roman Church

When Paul wrote to the Romans, he had not been involved with the planting or development of the church there, but he wrote to them, setting out his credentials and arguing cogently for the work he was doing. He wrote for their good, for he had been interested in them for years and had intended to come for some time (1.13; 15.22–24; 28–29). His desire was to pass on a spiritual benefit to them (1.11; 1.15) and to instruct them in their faith. There is much more, but the principle seems to be that it was for their benefit—another principle of accompaniment.

Question: Does a person have to be *present* to accompany a church, or can written and telephone contact be enough?

Agabus and Paul

When Agabus spoke to Paul in Caesarea about his future (Acts 21), he was already well known for his prophetic ministry (see Acts 11.28ff). So, when he warned Paul of impending imprisonment, there was little doubt in anyone's minds that it would happen as he said. Although Paul ignored the advice—it was his intention to go anyway—he was now fully aware of what was going to happen. I feel there are some lessons here for accompaniment:

- At times, it is necessary to speak out in such situations, especially when the message is clearly from God. (I am not saying that accompaniers are to be prophets!)

- It is the prerogative of the local church to decide whether to agree with the accompanier or not. The final decision always remains with the local situation. The accompanier can never be anything more than an adviser, even if it is clear to the accompanier that the group is going in the wrong direction.

Question: Is your church prepared for direct input from someone like Agabus? Will they listen?

Team work

These events described so briefly illustrate a biblical principle, that God uses groups of people to fulfil his purposes. So Paul describes the people of God as a body (Eph 4.16) in which each part does its work, and he always appointed a group of elders and not one on his own (Tit 1.5).

As we have seen he always worked with a group of people and even John Mark who was responsible for the falling out with Barnabas is later reconciled and works with Paul (Col 4.10, 2 Tim 4.11, Philemon 24). This is the way that God works too. Like Paul we can say that we are his fellow-workers (1 Cor 3.9, 2 Cor 6.1). Although he does not *need* us, he chooses to work in this way. Accompaniment by giving encouragement, telling the truth when it needs to be heard, and walking alongside are important elements of being fellow-workers with God and with each other.

Question: Who are the members of your team? Are you giving them encouragement, telling them the truth when they need to hear it and walking alongside them?

of depressing delays, and limited service, I think it is doubtful whether we would have been disciplined enough to carry out such a thorough review of our aims. We might have assumed that our original vision still held good without assessing whether or not it remains appropriate for contemporary needs in the community. He has helped us look for ways of handing on the original vision to the next generation of trustees and volunteers, while keeping it relevant to current circumstances.

Comment

I asked myself the question of whether the venture would have happened without the accompanier. It seems that at Bridges, John's presence has made the difference between success and failure. It remains to be seen how this will develop in the future when the accompaniment process ends — or perhaps it should not end…

In reflecting on the accompaniment process, John feels that it would be helpful if the accompanier were given a clearer picture of his or her role at commencement. I am sure he is right, but with the wide range of projects and the make-up of the group being accompanied, this may be an impossible task, for there will be significant variations in the role. However, mission accompaniment stands and falls in the matching of the right people to the situations. Not every relationship can or will work but so much depends on getting this right. Training and development together with growing skills in the process must help.

BBH accompaniers meet twice a year for briefing, training and support and attend a residential 'Future Church' conference. At these conferences, case studies are examined and themes explored where pilots and accompaniers with church leaders and mission enablers are stimulated towards imaginative praxis in their own setting. The Future Church conferences have enabled the trustees of Bridges to see a bigger picture and appreciate that they have been pioneers (with other groups around the UK) in getting church into the community.

I commend the process of mission accompaniment because it is:

- Ecumenical
- Long term
- Missional

An accompanier is able to see much more as he or she is not completely involved with the project and can often help the people involved to see reality far more than they would otherwise.

4 How Does Accompaniment Work?

The best way to understand the workings is to examine another story, this time of a very different Anglican church.

Much is being said and written about emerging churches—here is one such story.

Story 3: Harvest, a 'New Way of Being Church'

Story told by Tim Morgan, BBH Accompanier, lay Anglican and CMS Area Co-ordinator.

It was launched in 1998 as an officially sanctioned Church of England experiment within the Diocese of Canterbury. Harvest was not born as the result of 'transitioning' *in situ*, nor was it a 'church plant.' Rather it was a new movement, formed by a group of Christians following a fresh vision. About 50 people, under the leadership of Revd Kerry Thorpe (until then vicar of Holy Trinity, Margate), formed the original team whose goal was to set up a 'new way of being church.'

Harvest is a 'network church' and follows the principles of other cell churches in the UK and worldwide. There is no permanent church building and no geographical parish—the basic unit of church life is the small group, or cell (which means the people in the cell—not the cell meeting). Cells meet together weekly in homes (using the four Ws of Welcome, Worship, Word and Witness) and the whole church meets together for worship and teaching on a Sunday morning, currently on a college campus.

In its own words, 'Harvest has grown gently in faith, in experience and in numbers since that beginning.' Six years after its launch *Harvest* operates through ten cells, which together number around 80 people.

The BBH accompaniment with Harvest began in December 2002 at the request of Kerry Thorpe, with a view to:

1 Addressing the following questions:

    a) What is the next step of our development?

    b) How do we continue to grow?

c) Should we plant again?

d) How do we maintain a momentum for personal and spiritual growth?

2 Exploring the following core BBH indicators:

a) Sharing Faith and Values

b) Nourishing Daily Living

c) Becoming Communities of Learning

The initial plan was to meet bi-monthly with the Core Team (which consisted of Kerry as Senior Minister, plus the four Cell Coaches), occasionally with the Reference Group (chaired by the Bishop of Maidstone), and to attend other groups and meetings and meet with individuals as appropriate. A report of no more than one side of A4 would be produced after each meeting. The accompaniment was set to last two years.

The main focus of the first year of accompaniment was a series of meetings with the Core Team. No meetings were set up specially—rather a BBH component was fitted in to existing meetings. It was at three of these meetings with the Cell Coaches that the three chosen BBH indicators were discussed in turn. This involved an exploration rather than a presentation of the themes—a dialogue not a monologue. As each of the indicators chosen was already to some degree a strength of Harvest, there was a considerable amount of agreement and a sense of moving together in the same direction. This was a confirmation that the leaders were all 'singing from the same hymn sheet'…if that is not an inappropriate term for a church that uses an overhead projector for its corporate worship times!

The main focus of the first year of accompaniment was a series of meetings with the Core Team

The second year of accompaniment has so far involved attendance at a Sunday morning meeting (where the accompanier had an opportunity to preach) and visits to midweek meetings of three of the cells (which the accompanier simply joined as a member of the group). This section of the accompaniment has been less easy to report on, but has been valuable for the accompanier in terms of getting a 'feel' for the church, its members, and the 'spiritual temperature.'

The final six months of the accompaniment will see a return to meeting with the Core Team in order to review progress on the issues discussed during the first year, and to explore some of the remaining BBH indicators.

It is, due to its rather enigmatic, hands-off, just-ask-questions nature, a little difficult to assess how helpful or otherwise the accompaniment has been. Likewise, any measurement of the 'successes' and 'failures' is somewhat elusive. However, there have been positive reactions to the stimulus of some of the discussions in the Core Team meetings, and a general agreement that being accompanied is a 'good thing.' The remaining period of accompaniment will hopefully see a number of threads coming together, and the process is open enough to be extended if both accompanier and pilot deem it beneficial.

The seven BBH indicators have been helpful as an investigative tool

The seven BBH indicators (six if you exclude 'willingness to be accompanied') have been helpful as an investigative tool. The three used so far have all opened up interesting avenues of discussion and exploration, but as already mentioned these three were already associated with areas of strength in Harvest. During the concluding period of accompaniment it will be interesting to explore one or two of the other indicators—not because they may or may not be areas of strength for Harvest, but because they were not originally chosen.

From the accompanier's point of view it has been fascinating to follow the evolving journey of such an unusual experiment in the context of the Church of England. Furthermore, as opportunities present themselves for sharing the Harvest story more widely, the BBH process will enable churches and movements around the country to learn from the joys and disappointments, the frustrations and the challenges that *Harvest* has faced along the way. And that can only be a good thing.

Comment

This story illustrates the difference between the various pilot projects, and the way accompaniment has been worked through—there can be no enforced pattern that will work everywhere. There are differences between the four nations involved (England, Scotland, Ireland and Wales) and every situation must be treated as the individual group that they are. However, there are agreed ways of working and this is worth looking at next.

Setting up the Accompaniment 5

The process begins with an initial discussion between BBH staff and the potential pilot.

Part of this process is to identify a mutually agreed accompanier who will enter into a contract with both the pilot and BBH. This is deliberately an ecumenical process. The accompanier will be deliberately chosen to have a different background and churchmanship to the potential pilot. Thus the accompanier, who will have his or her own skills to bring to the work, comes without the knowledge and understanding of the jargon used and will have to ask questions just to understand what is going on. This is the significant difference with BBH mission accompaniment to other forms of coaching, mentoring and mission consultancy.

Accompaniers are not left on their own to get on with it, but are encouraged and supported throughout the process. BBH has regular briefing and training throughout the process. A major part of the process is through learning from other accompaniers as they come together regularly.

The contract is for a long-term but fixed period — open-ended agreements are not a part of *this* process — the most suitable period is usually between 18 and 30 months. The intention is that regular meetings between the accompanier and the pilot will take place at most every 8 weeks.

The work then begins *together*. There is a common framework for discussion using some or all of the seven key learning indicators, but each accompanier and pilot will tailor this to their own situation. Through discussion and questioning, the team begins to build a relationship and the work.

BBH is committed to assisting churches in their expression of *mission*. They have tested accompaniment from the local church, to regional bodies to national denominational executives and have found that the skilful outside, impartial, client-centred approach using creative open questioning, visiting regularly over a longer period of time, becomes a visible sign of the wider church. Prayerfully and spiritually, an accompanier can enable new pathways and opportunities, reveal strengths previously missed and give courage to stay focused on God's vision, as the Emmaus Road story transformed the disciples. The skilful outsider gently and purposefully can transform churches with confidence into mission.

6

What Does the Mission Accompanier Do?

The diversity amongst the pilots has already been stressed, but the role of the accompaniers can be summarized as follows:

1 **Listen**—the agenda of the pilot is the only agenda, so a careful listening is the only way it can work.
2 **Reflect**—it can be helpful to reflect back to the participants what is being said (and not said), to ensure that everyone has a clear understanding.
3 **Question**—the key concerns can usually be discovered by careful questioning.
4 **Discuss**—an 'outsider' (who gradually becomes an insider too) can often lead a discussion to unblock the thinking of the group, having themselves identified that this is a problem.
5 **Signpost**—the wider knowledge of the accompanier and the networking with other accompaniers will often give insights for sources of specific help.
6 **Interpret**—someone who is not immediately involved with a project can often present it in a clearer light to others.
7 **Facilitate**—this aspect is very important as it enables the group to work, reflect and pray.

So, the role involves a level of participation as well as simply observing, but there are some boundaries relating to training and consultancy. These will need to be understood and agreed on by both sides. Underlying everything else is the requirement for discretion, confidentiality and teamwork—with the project and other accompaniers.

Story 4: Mission Accompaniment in Tallaght

Story told by Fred Graham, recently retired. BBH Accompanier and Church of Ireland Minister.

Tallaght, an area of severe social deprivation, lies on the southern edge of Dublin City and has a population of 120,000 people. Over the last 20 years, a new Methodist church has developed from a meeting of local people in a home, culminating in May 2004 when a new church and community building was opened. In the autumn of 2001, this small congregation became involved with BBH. They were involved in much work, but there was no local church committee or council and the work of the church was largely in the hands of a church worker with volunteer help, and supervised by the local circuit superintendent.

A new reference group was set up comprising the church worker, the local circuit superintendent, members of the local church, a lay member of the circuit and two members of the BBH steering group in Ireland. This reference group explored their vision, purposes and values, reviewed their strengths, weaknesses, opportunities and threats and drew up a broad development plan listing the various responsibilities and priorities facing the church. In April 2003, a church council was set up in Tallaght comprising members of the reference group with additional local and circuit members. Fred writes:

> The role of accompanier is both challenging and fulfilling. Accompaniers were asked not to act as consultants or trainers but as an objective presence, a critical friend who sat alongside people as they managed their affairs and piloted a way into the future. There were resources available to us. There were the seven learning areas gleaned from the action-research in the earlier stage of the BBH process. There was our own experience, also the support of the BBH staff and insights gained from twice-yearly training events and the annual conference.
>
> How effective was the work of the accompanier? I believe that the very presence of an accompanier was helpful to the reference group. It affirmed the value of their work together and helped them to adopt a more objective approach to their work.
>
> The process of struggling together to determine their vision, values and purposes not only helped the group to lay the foundation for priorities and a strategy, it also bonded them together as a group and deepened their commitment to the mission of the church.
>
> Regarding the future, it is hoped that when the term of accompaniment under the BBH project finishes, Tallaght Church will engage another accompanier. This would be in line with the recommendation of the Connexions Report currently being implemented in the Methodist Church in Ireland that all local congregations should be accompanied.

Some Comments from Tallaght Methodist Church

Our starting aims were:

- to build a dynamic team of workers to meet the spiritual, emotional and physical needs of the community both inside and outside the church group;
- to attract people into the worshipping community;
- to become financially independent and support our own church and community building.

Our accompanier joined a small vision group that met monthly. He observed these meetings and then shared his thoughts on the group. Encouraging discussion, he focused this group into a steering committee that looked at the vision values and purpose of our church in order to meet the needs of our community in Tallaght. He also shared some biblical teaching that encouraged, strengthened and enabled us to go forward with our aims. Looking back over the last few years we can see those aims have been met and are still being built on. We have to be reminded of our vision, values and purposes every now and again and our accompanier is very good at doing that.

When our accompanier joined us, we were a haphazard group of very different people from different backgrounds who had no plan of action but with a heart and desire to do something in our community. BBH has helped to mould us into an effective fellowship of people who are making a real impact on our local community. It has helped to turn us from a small house group into a structured church fellowship. We now have a working multi-purpose built church, which consists of a chapel, a sports hall, six meeting rooms, and a reflective garden. We are developing a more structured youth programme, hold weekly Sunday Services, regular Bible studies and a mother and toddler group, and have community outreach programmes including keep fit classes and a support group for those living with drug and alcohol dependencies. Soon we hope to develop a partnership with the YMCA working with disadvantaged local parents and kids. We will soon be facilitating the neighbouring health centre with rooms for programmes including ante-natal classes, parent craft and health education.

We have come a long way with BBH and in a very short space of time and are very grateful to the helping hand it has given us. BBH has enabled us to attain the position we are in much quicker than we ever would have been able to achieve ourselves. It is questionable whether we would have actually been able to achieve it at all without BBH and the mission accompanier.

BBH has given us structure and strength—it has empowered and inspired, focused and encouraged us!

Comment

Can Accompaniment be Improved?

It certainly can! BBH has been a learning process and much that is good has been learnt and put into practice, but the learning cannot be finished yet. From Tallaght have come two suggestions:

- It may have been helpful to have the accompanier spend a period of time observing the day to day work of the church life in action, rather than just hear reports back of the work done.

- More visual techniques could have been an added advantage. Sometimes documentation could be too detailed, complicated, or confusing for people to digest.

To that we might add:

- Accompaniers could be better prepared by knowing more of the group and what is expected of them before they start, as John Ledger suggested earlier.

- The key to the future will be two-fold:
  - ◊ providing excellent training for prospective accompaniers;
  - ◊ transferring the skills gained for matching the accompanier with the group, so that many more can be involved in the process.

Fred Graham's comment is especially apt:

The form that accompaniment takes is determined by many factors, including the type of group, the nature of its work and the skills and experience of the accompanier. However, the BBH project has shown that accompaniment (in most cases) can be an encouraging and sup-portive presence to local and regional church bodies as they reflect on their mission.

Reflecting further on the biblical material (see centre pull-out section), what has struck me the most is the contrast between our tendency towards isolation and the biblical pattern of working together. Perhaps we would not need ac-companiment if we always worked in partnership with others! I have found these verses quite a challenge to my own work and ministry, and feel that the principle is reflected in the stories above.

7

Conclusion

How can my Church Use this Process?

I was convinced that outside help was necessary before I began writing, but the more I have thought through and written the more I am convinced that we all need a Jethro or Paul to mentor us as Jesus would. All of us as church leaders need accompaniers, just as individuals—especially new converts—need them, but so do churches and organizations. BBH has something valuable to teach us, but only as it becomes a part of mainstream church life.

Do you have a spiritual director and does your congregation? Is it time to consider approaching someone?

The BBH mission accompaniment process offers churches and organizations:

- Ideas to test and develop *ie* the seven learning indicators
- Skilled, sensitive and disciplined accompaniment
- A developing network with other innovators or developers
- Signposting to other sources of support included with the training
- Recognition as part of an ecumenical experiment in new ways of doing mission

No one is suggesting that this is a perfect process, but it is a developing one. Mission accompaniment is the most important part of the BBH process and is a lesson to be learned in other processes. We are continually learning this with Natural Church Development.

I believe that this is the time to lose our isolationism and self-sufficiency and learn from the New Testament that others accompanying us in our process of change to becoming a missional church will enable us to be more effective in that change process. The greatest obstacle is the resistance of church leaders and church members to recognize that being open to a Mission Accompanier is far less threatening than the alternative—a slow death and closure!

Will it work for you? I am sure that it will, just as those who have been a part of it so far have found that it did, but it takes spiritual maturity and courage to do it. There is a great deal of fear and reticence to involve an outsider in the work, but those that do reap great benefit.

You need to ask yourself 'What might someone different see with fresh eyes as they accompany me?' An accompanier does not come to criticize, but ask the obvious and (sometimes) silly questions like the Court Jester of old. Often, they will ask the questions others would like to ask, but they do not dare because they would look foolish. The stories above show that much of the work of an accompanier is to reflect and *encourage* you, and these need to be held together.

Would you not welcome a fresh perspective in your situation? Do you get the feeling that you are failing to see the wood for the trees? What will happen in your church, if you consider mission accompaniment in your situation? Will the mission of your church change? It would be a great challenge, but is that not what leadership is all about?

Appendix: What of the Future?

BBH is an action-research project of the Churches' Commission on Mission, Churches Together in Britain and Ireland. This current phase will end in March 2006. Some 31 pilot projects across Britain and Ireland have been deployed across the church traditions accompanied by men and women, ordained and lay across a wide church affiliation.

'Mission accompaniment' is the legacy of BBH coupled with a methodology using the BBH seven learning indicators of a mission church, with a distinctive style that is contextual and concerned for mature discipleship by churches.

BBH is due to launch in September 2005 through Cliff College, Derbyshire a validated Diploma in Mission Accompaniment. This two-year (part time) distance-learning course can provide a means for training future accompaniers in the BBH process.

It is hoped that a Fellowship, College or Society of Mission Accompaniers will develop both to provide regional training to people as well as developing best practices in accompaniment, standards of behaviour and a list of recommended accompaniers/mission consultants.

Further, it is hoped to assess and refine the methodology of accompaniment, so that specialist fields may develop. In addition, refinement of the seven learning indicators applied to both historic church patterns as well as fresh ways of being church.

Written and web-based resources are being developed, for example *Changing Churches*.[7] These will provide access points to understand how others have sought to revitalize and develop mission engagement and be an entry point for those in leadership to consider the option.

Self-development by churches who appoint their own accompaniers will be part of the future with more web and written materials available on how to appoint your own mission accompanier, including the qualities and skills required and how to define areas for accompaniment and draw up a working agreement.

Focal persons will be available as regional points of contact to provide information, and there will be taster days for churches and tools from church and community auditing, networks of resources and an executive of matchmakers to match mission accompaniers to churches.

Contacts

Building Bridges of Hope
Address: CTBI, Bastille Court, 2 Paris Garden, London SE1 8ND
Tel: 020 7654 7236
Email: bbh@ctbi.org.uk
Web site: www.ccom.org.uk/bbh
Weblog: http://buildingbridges.blogspot.com

Cliff College
Address: Cliff College, Hope Valley, Calver, Sheffield S32 3XG
Tel: 01246 584220
Email: info@cliff.college.ac.uk
Web site: www.cliffcollege.ac.uk

Notes

1   Jim Currin, *How to Develop a Mission Strategy* (Grove Evangelism booklet, Ev68).

2   See Mike Booker, *Exploring Natural Church Development* (Grove Evangelism booklet, Ev55).

3   CYTÛN is the Welsh equivalent of Churches Together in England.

4   Captain Phillip Johansson, Chief Secretary of Church Army, at a speech to Church Army Conference 1999.

5   *Leadership,* Vol XXV, Number 2, pp 46–7, italics mine.

6   Matthew records one of these events (17.1) and Luke records two (8.51; 9.28). In Mark 13.3, Andrew joins the other three in questioning Jesus.

7   Jeanne Hinton, *Changing churches: building bridges for local mission* (CTBI 2002); Jeanne Hinton and Peter Price, *Changing communities: church from the grassroots* (CTBI 2003); Stuart Murray, *Changing mission: learning from newer churches* (CTBI 2005); Philip Knights, *Changing evangelisation: learning from the Catholic experience* (CTBI 2005/6). Further planned titles: Simon Barrow and Terry Tennens, *Changing people: learning mission accompaniment* (CTBI 2006); *Changing places: re-learning mission shaped church* (CTBI 2007).